The

Knock

Copyright©2018

All Rights Reserved

Publisher: Tommy Arbuckle Ministries

Author: Tommy L. Arbuckle III

ISBN: 978-1-7320085-0-2

Printed in the USA by: Digital Publishing of Florida http://www.digitalpubfl.com

From The Author

_____

_____

_____

_____

_____

_____

_____

_____

_____

_____

_____

About The Author

Tommy Arbuckle is a prophetic teacher, intercessor, entrepreneur and mentor called by God to be a leader in both business and ministry. He's a recipient of the *"40 Leaders under Forty Award"* in business and is a ruling Elder in his church; *"Judah International Ministries"* located in Mackinaw, Illinois where he also serves as *Chief Armorbearer* to *Archbishop Mark A. DuBois.*

He's a native of Houston, Texas. He received his Bachelor's degree in Electrical Engineering from the Historically Black College of Prairie View A&M University in Prairie View, Texas. Tommy owns a general contracting company, *AFE Construction, LLC* and is a builder of not only commercial and residential properties but a builder of people through mentoring and ministry.

Tommy is uniquely gifted in the area of street and marketplace evangelism where healings, miracles, signs and wonders follow him. He's passionate about seeing each member within the Body of Christ walking in the fullness of their measure and being about the Father's business.

Tommy is married and has six (6) daughters and resides in Peoria, Illinois. In his free time, he loves to hunt and fish.

Acknowledgements & Dedications

Over the years, I've been blessed to have many influencers which I call my *"tutors and governors"* *Galatians 4:2 (KJV)* who have been some of the hands and voices from God in my life. **Archbishop Mark Dubois**, you're truly a father to the fatherless. **Apostle Eric Newble**, where would I be without the voice of inspiration in your breath, dream…. Dreamer! **Dr. Freddie Frazier**, you took an interest in me when everyone else said *"He's not worth your time."* May the crowns of glory on your head shine brighter than all the consolation in the heavens.

To my wife Monica and daughters Destiny, Kiara, Moriah, Olivia, Sylvia and Victoria thanks for your continual support in my pursuit of God for our family.

To my team specialists Jean Logan, Pamela Thomas and Darryl Brown, I appreciate the godly gifts in you and your willingness to use them for His glory.

I would like to dedicate this book to my Father, Tommy L. Arbuckle, Sr. who introduced me to God at a very young age. Walking into his bedroom one evening as a child and asking him what book he was reading, which happened to be the Bible, became the very foundation I stand on today. Though his transition into glory was early on my timeline, what he imparted by reading the Bible to me nightly would remain with me and our family for all of eternity.

Introduction

Luke 4:18-19 "The Spirit of the Lord is upon me, because he hath anointed me to preach the gospel to the poor; he hath sent me to heal the brokenhearted, to preach deliverance to the captives, and recovering of sight to the blind, to set at liberty them that are bruised, To preach the acceptable year of the Lord" (KJV).

In these scriptures we discover the reason why Jesus was so compelled to preach the gospel. We find that God anointed Him and because of this anointing, the Spirit of the Lord rested upon Him. Jesus used these scriptures out of the book of Isaiah as an announcement to the Jews in the city of Nazareth. He was raised in Nazareth and His ministry was also birthed there. Jesus was sent to preach the gospel to the poor, heal the brokenhearted, preach deliverance to the captives and recovering of sight to the blind, **to set at liberty them that are bruised** and preach the acceptable year of the Lord. In our lives, we often take hits from a variety of things which can result in bruises. The word bruised in this scripture means there are things that can happen in our lives which might not break the skin, but you definitely know it happened by the resulting mark it leaves. When these bruises occur, they can be very painful but we still try to proceed forward in life not knowing the bruise itself has us on a self-imposed lockdown. For this reason, **Jesus is knocking.**

Table of Contents

> *God will never give you more than you can take. He will let you bend but He will NEVER let you break......*
>
> *Author Unknown*

Chapter

1

Have you ever been woken up by a knocking sound and wondered where it was coming from? Your first thought or reaction is someone might be at your door. You don't move immediately because you're waiting for the knocking to continue to make sure of what you heard. If the sound doesn't continue you fall back to sleep but if it persists, you get up to find the source of the knocking and who or what is knocking. At this moment the knocking has gained your attention. Sometimes you're not asleep and there's a knocking sound and again your reaction is to find the source of *"The Knock."* In *Revelation 3:20*, Jesus says: *"Behold, I stand at the door and knock" (KJV).* He's not referring to a sound you hear with your natural ears, it's a knock on the doors of your heart. He's knocking because He wants to come in and <u>sup</u> with you. If you know anything about the historical context of having <u>supped</u> with a person; it's symbolic of a very personal and close relationship developed by spending time together eating and talking. I often hear people talk about how they're seeking God to get close to Him, but in this passage of scripture, Jesus is the one doing the seeking. He loves you so much that He takes the initiative to come to where you are, so you don't have to look for Him. **Jesus is knocking** because He's trying to gain your attention. He wants to commune with you and *"The Knock"* isn't something you should disregard; it's going to require a response from you. *"The Knock"* at the door is literally a decision on your part to respond to the sound. You hear it, but will you move to open it? There are times God will awake you early in the morning, you may not respond to the awakening like He wants, but God isn't easily deterred. You must understand *"The Knock"* is a decision you must make to answer the call to intimacy. It's a call for you to draw near, to come closer to God. You may or may not be a Christian but the question I pose to you is **"Have you made the decision to allow God to have access to all areas of your life, even the parts you've closed off?"** For Christians, you want Him as your Lord and Savior, so you let Him come into your life but in the back of your mind, you're saying *"Lord, you can't go in this room or that room."* You're very selective to where God can have access to or dwell in.

"The Knock" is also a call for healing, deliverance and unmasking. When Jesus is at the door, He's knocking to assist you in discovering who you really are or in some cases, uncover who you're pretending to be.

"The Knock" is a call for love. It's literally a call for love out of **OBEDIENCE** to His word. You must be willing to obey Him and when you do, according to scripture, *"If anyone loves me, he will obey my word, and my Father will love him, and we will come to him and take up residence with him" John 14:23 (NET).*

God wants to dwell in your heart and life to bring healing and restoration, but He can only do it if you open the door of your heart and let Him in. In order for this to transpire, you must answer *"THE KNOCK!"*

How have you responded to "The Knock?"

_____

_____

_____

_____

_____

_____

_____

_____

_____

_____

_____

_____

_____

> *God still listens, answers, heals, forgives, leads, directs, cares and loves...*

Chapter

2

Gates and doors found throughout the Bible scriptures denote places of access. Doors keep things in and they also keep things out. Jesus can easily walk through the door but He wants to be invited in. *"The Doors"* Jesus wants to enter are closed doors that were once open. You closed those doors and unknowingly put a wall between you and Jesus. He's outside that door wanting to gain access because these doors are the entryway into your life. It's by faith you open *"The Doors"* of your heart to Jesus. You're responsible for your actions and this passage of scripture holds you accountable. Only you get to decide if the door will be opened, Jesus won't break the door down to gain entry, He'll **NEVER** force Himself upon you. If you want Jesus to come in and <u>sup</u> with you, it depends on whether or not you respond to *"The Knock"* and open the door.

These doors are not physical in nature, they're hidden inside your heart. They're locked up by things like: anger, frustration, shame, unforgiveness, fear and self-condemnation. They have been locked as a result of the hits and bruises you have taken over the course of your life. *John 16:33,* states: *"In the world you will have tribulation" (KJV).* This scripture lets you know you'll get knocked down and sometimes bruised by the world, but Jesus finishes this verse by saying: *"Be of good cheer, for I have overcome the world."* While Jesus may have overcome the world, you're still hurting from the pain, affliction and bruises that have been inflicted upon you. This has caused you to surround yourself with walls or locked doors and you won't allow access through them. It's a self-defense mechanism to guard against any further damage but it's causing you more harm than good. What you haven't anticipated is what's on the other side of those walls and doors is why Jesus is knocking. He knows in order for you to be **COMPLETE,** you must let down those walls you have encased yourself with. While they're there to guard against outside forces, they have actually imprisoned you. Sure, *Proverbs 4:23 (KJV)* tells you to **"*guard your heart*"** but you have shielded these areas from the **ONLY** person who can ratify the problem. Jesus stands there and continues to knock because He wants to bring healing and deliverance.

Remember, **"*The Knock*"** is an invitation for you and God to commune together. It's an invitation to allow Him access into the hidden and hurt parts of your life. The question is, will you open **"*The Doors*"** of your heart and let Him in?

Identify the locked doors in your life?

_____

_____

_____

_____

_____

_____

_____

_____

_____

_____

_____

_____

_____

God, you have my permission to break every chain holding me hostage in my life...

Chapter

3

"Blessed is the man that heareth me, watching daily at my gates, waiting at the posts of my doors" **Proverbs 8:34 (KJV)**.

To **hear** means: to open one's heart, it has nothing to do with your eardrums. The hearing of Jesus' knock is provisional because when Jesus talks about hearing, it can pose a problem. When God spoke to Jesus in **John 12:29** there were different accounts of what people heard. It states: **"The people therefore, that stood by, and heard it, said that it thundered: others said, An angel spake to him" (KJV).** Could it be you don't recognize His knock? What you heard; did you attribute it to something else? We all hear in many different ways; God communicates in different ways as well. What and how you hear is dependent on the frequency you tune into. For some of us, it comes in dreams and visions or a prophetic word. Others it may be a television commercial, songs on the radio or a sign you see on a billboard. You can become very selective in your hearing and choose to ignore sometimes what's obvious to your godly senses. How could this happen? You've taken hard hits in your journey that left you with bruises.

In the scriptures, the word **bruise** means: **there's been some things that have occurred in your life that has caused you pain**. The remembrance of that pain has kept you from hearing and recognizing Jesus knocking. Although the bruises didn't break your skin, they left a mark reminding you of the event that caused the pain. The bruise has set in and has become extremely sore, to touch it is a reminder of how you obtained it. So, what do you do? You put a **DO NOT ENTER** sign on the door because of the bruise and sealed the door shut. Over time certain things don't work well for you because you carry signs of the event that's noticeable to everyone you encounter. They know something happened to you, but they also know not to ask about it because it could be very sensitive in nature. Although the event that caused the bruise is over, you carry an aura about yourself that lets the world know something is going on and it's not up for discussion. You know what happened, you've held onto it for years. You don't recognize it's causing a disruption in your life because you've grown so accustomed to being shielded that you're not aware of it. Jesus wants to gain access to those areas but you haven't taken the necessary steps or action to respond to His invitation. There's a deafening in your spirit that's causing you to not **HEAR "*THE KNOCK!*"**

What bruises caused you to not hear The Knock?

_____

_____

_____

_____

_____

_____

_____

_____

_____

_____

_____

God has a purpose for your pain, a reason for your struggle and a reward for your faith...

Chapter

4

Chapter 4   "Hindrances To Answering The Knock"

You want to be obedient and answer **"The Knock"** but sometimes things get in the way. You've been trodden down from the offenses you have taken. The word **trodden** in *Luke 8:5* means: **to crush or to offend.** *Luke 17:1* states: *"Then said he unto the disciples, It is impossible but that offences will come: but woe unto him, through whom they come" (KJV).* When you have an experience that's crushing, it causes you not to hear.

When I was in elementary school, a girl passed me a note telling me she liked me. The teacher saw it and made us both go around to other teachers (her friends) classrooms and stand in front of the entire class saying *"We loved each other."* All of the students were laughing, the teachers were laughing but inside I was embarrassed. I'm sure the girl didn't fair out as well either from the public humiliation as I remember her crying uncontrollably. For me, this incident caused a bruise in my soul and it crushed me. It was a very painful situation that I never told my parents about and had forgotten until a prophet of God came up to me one day after a church service. He said: *"The Lord said something happened to you as a child that caused you hurt and made you to feel ashamed and you've closed off that area of your life."* I said: *"No, I'm good, I'm alright, I don't know what you're talking about."* I actually thought he was in error with his words, I tried to move away from him but he persisted.

As I began to ponder what he was saying, the Lord showed me how that one incident caused a blockage in my life that I was unaware of in my walk with Him. There was a closed door in my life that I blocked off which could've caused me **to not let Jesus in when He came knocking to set me free**. I was offended by the event in elementary school and never wanted to talk about it again. *Proverbs 18:19 states: "A brother offended is harder to be won than a strong city and their contentions are like the bars of a castle" (KJV).* But that day, I opened the door of my heart and allowed Jesus inside to heal that little boy who was made to feel ashamed.

You may have experienced and/or encountered similar things. If you begin to look over your life, you'll find places you've "walled off" or have placed a **DO NOT ENTER** sign because of past offenses. You have "self-layered" yourself like Adam and Eve did in the garden by sewing fig leaves to cover themselves. It may be your work, title, prestige or things you do which you've tried to use to keep yourself covered up to avoid the conversation. It's because of those areas, **Jesus is knocking**.

Maybe your door has been abused or maybe it has been mistreated so you're reluctant to open it. Perhaps you felt like no one wants to use your door, so you simply have stopped being attentive to it or looking for someone to inquire about access through it.

The devil knows there are territories you're destined and designed to walk in. His job is to keep you locked inside the walls of your heart so you'll never occupy those places. When you hear *"The Knock"* and fail to arise or move to allow Jesus access into those areas, you've closed off yourself and the cycle of imprisonment continues. Your life is one big house with many rooms and while Jesus is on the outside trying to get in, it's up to you as to whether you'll allow Him access. Once you accept Him as your Savior, He'll come in but He wants to do more than come in the foyer of your life. He wants to fellowship with you in every room along with every experience. When you accepted Him as your Savior, you invited Him in, you must continue to let Him in to other areas of your life. You were seeking access to Him, only now He's the one seeking access into your entire life.

Pain, frustration, disappointments, shame, guilt, unforgiveness and humiliation are some of the hindrances that keeps you locked in. Jesus is seeking access so He can deliver you from **YOU**. Will you let Him in?

Chapter

5

In **Revelation 3:20**, Jesus gives a condition on who can answer **"The Knock."** In it He states: **"If any man hears my voice"** **(KJV).** The problem with this statement is you may hear Him but you may not understand exactly what you're hearing.

There are things you'll hear and see from God that you won't understand what it means. Why does God do that? Why would God say something to us knowing we don't understand what He's saying? It's a call to intimacy, a call to come **sup** with Him, a call to seek Him for the answers. There are times when God will speak to me in **WORDS,** not a dialogue or pictures, just a single word. God has spoken words to me that I've never heard before which would send me to a dictionary to understand it. I'll give you an example. I had a dream one night and when I woke up from the dream, I couldn't remember the contents of it. I tried to remember what I dreamed about but for the life of me I couldn't. I began asking God what was the dream about because I wanted to write it down. After inquiring several times with Him to help me remember the dream, I saw in the spirit the word **"Manasseh"** flash three times. What I mean by seeing in the spirit is my physical eyes were open when this happened, not closed, but I could clearly see the word overlay what I was seeing with my natural eyes. Because it flashed three times, I remembered each of the letters of the word so I started spelling it out then I pronounced it.

Manasseh was a word I heard before and I knew Manasseh was a descendant of the tribes of Israel but I didn't understand why I saw it. So, I looked up the word in a dictionary and was surprised when I found out what it meant. The word Manasseh means **"causing to forget."** In *Genesis 41:51,* it explains why Joseph named his son Manasseh. It states: ***"And Joseph called the name of the firstborn Manasseh: For God, said he, hath made me forget all my toil, and all my father's house" (KJV).*** From the definition and scripture, I understood that it was God that caused me to forget the dream. He didn't want me to remember it and after more inquiring of God; I found the dream wasn't from God but from the devil, therefore God caused me not to remember it.

When you further read **Revelation 3:20**, you find two scenarios which must occur before Jesus can come in and <u>sup</u> with you. The first one deals with your ability to hear. God says: ***"If any man will hear my voice."*** He's not questioning your ability to hear but your **WILLINGNESS** to hear and **OBEY**. This particular hearing has nothing to do with your natural hearing, but it concerns your spiritual hearing. ***"The Knock"*** at the door gets your attention, the question is: do you hear it and will you respond to it?

The second scenario requires you to make a **DECISION**. For He says, ***"If any man will open the door."*** He gives you an invitation to invite Him in, He waits for your consent to enter. This is the correct order of God because you can't open if you don't hear; you'll be hesitant to make a decision to answer if you don't know who's knocking. What's amazing to me is Jesus doesn't say anything about someone hearing Him knocking, only you must **HEAR HIS VOICE.** This denotes a relationship of the truest kind in order to know who's talking simply by their voice.

Many have knocked on the door of your heart and you opened without knowing who was there to later find out they were wolves in sheep clothing. Jesus reminds us in *John 14:28, "My sheep hear My voice, and I know them, and they follow me" (KJV).* Do you have that type of relationship with Jesus where you know His voice and how to respond when **HE KNOCKS?**

Chapter

6

The Pharisees were the teachers of the law and the Scribes copied the scriptures. You would think the ones teaching and copying the scriptures would know Jesus as the Messiah when He showed up but they didn't. This proves you can teach and write the scriptures but you don't have true knowledge or a relationship with Him. In **John 4:49** Jesus says: ***"Search the scriptures; for in them ye think ye have eternal life: and they are they which testify of me"*** *(KJV).* I know people who said they read the Bible in one year but can't tell you anything significant about what they read. The fact is; all they did was read. It's one thing to read a book about somebody but it's another thing to know them personally. It's one thing when others tell you what God is saying but when you can **HEAR** Him for yourself, that means you have developed a relationship; you **KNOW HIM!** Paraphrasing, *John 10:1-5,* Jesus is saying ***"His sheep know His voice and strangers they do not follow"***. If you know Him, you'll know His voice!

Anyone can knock on your door but it doesn't mean you're going to open it right away. When they **IDENTIFY** themselves, you'll move with haste because you know them. Jesus is not only knocking; He has identified Himself. You can't be set to do things your way in your own timing. This frame of mindset only shows you haven't transitioned or matured beyond the place where you first came to accept Him. Have you spent enough time in His presence to really know His voice? Knowing His voice births in you an understanding of His ways so you can make the transition beyond the walls that have kept you bound? Jesus is knocking and you keep saying **"Wait a minute, I'm not ready yet."** The problem with this is you'll spend your entire life trying to **"clean up your mess"** and that's not what Jesus wants. He's at the door **KNOCKING** saying *"I'll come in, let me do that for you."* He'll bring redemption to you and clean you up but you must first **HEAR HIS VOICE.** *Hebrews 3:15* states: *"If you will hear His voice, harden not your hearts, as in the provocation" (KJV).* You can call this an **"if"** scenario because **IF** you can hear His voice, you have spent enough time with Him to **KNOW** when He's speaking.

As mentioned earlier, hearing the voice of God and knowing His voice are two different things. When we don't understand something, we'll make a mistake and do something called **"presume."** Presume means "to think that something is true without actually knowing that it is." Do you find yourself being presumptuous? When He speaks to us in ways we don't understand, it's really a call for us to draw closer. *Proverb 25:2* states: *"It is the glory of God to conceal a thing; but the honour of kings is to search out a matter."* Remember, *"The Knock"* is a call for **INTIMACY.** God delights Himself in us spending time with Him. When we have an encounter or experience with God, we may see a picture or vision in our Spirit but we may not understand what we're hearing or seeing. Instead of drawing near to Him, we may run hastily to another believer in Christ to tell them what God did but may not know why or what He meant by what He did. We do this because there's something in us that likes to "presume" or act as though we know but in actuality, we don't. This behavior is not of God but rooted in pride and a product of our flesh nature. The devil further exploits this weakness to cause us to sin against God. You see this in *Genesis 3:1-8* where the devil tempts Adam and Eve. It was never about what fruit not to eat or to eat but an opportunity for them to learn from the Father by asking Him what's good and evil. The end result of them avoiding this conversation and relationship development resulted in their sinning and hiding from God; a symbol of immaturity.

How has Jesus revealed His voice to you?

_____

_____

_____

_____

_____

_____

_____

_____

_____

_____

_____

_____

_____

_____

_____

> *Hearing and knowing God's voice is essential to building an intimate relationship with Him. Not knowing His voice makes us vulnerable to the enemy's attacks and deception...*
>
> *Author Unknown*

Chapter

7

As I stated earlier, we all hear differently and we all grow at different stages. There are so many things you haven't seen or heard but God has prepared them because you have fallen in love with Him. Yet, there's a process you must go through called the **"Process of Maturation."** *Galatians 4:1* states: *"Now I say, That the heir, as long as he is a child, differeth nothing from a servant, though he be lord of all"* *(KJV).* Though we're called to reign and to rule, as long as we're in a place of immaturity, we'll never get there. It's a decision we must make. It's a decision of will you stay in the place where you are or will you move? Will you answer the door and allow Jesus into those locked places that's hindering your growth? You must understand that your doors and experiences have value.

In *Genesis 1:2 "...the earth was without form and void..."* *(KJV);* it was waiting for the **Spirit of God** to move and for God to speak into the darkness to call light out of it. You may not realize it but so many lives are depending on your **OPEN DOORS,** God is calling forth light out of your dark places. You may not believe you have worth and the risk is too great but there's a lot at stake if you don't open your doors and allow Him access. You'll never occupy the place God has designed for you to occupy if you don't grow past where you are and allow **HIM** access through all your doors.

If you could see in the Spirit, you would see the decision to allow Him into all areas of your life is your calling. It's what you were made to be and do. In the words of **Archbishop Mark Dubois** *"You have to be history sensitive but destiny focused."* Can you see it? You were made to sit in heavenly places with Christ Jesus, far above principalities and powers and rulers. Maybe when you look at your life and consider the events that happened, you muse about your life as a bridge to someone else. Because you've been double-crossed, you don't want anyone to cross your bridge again. I'm here to encourage you and to let you know that God's desire is for you to lift up your head. **Psalms 24:9** states: **"Lift up your head O ye gates and be ye lifted up ye everlasting doors and the King of Glory shall come in" (KJV).** You may ask yourself, if you don't open the door and allow Jesus access, what's at stake? What's at stake is your ability to rule as His son. Not only is it about being a believer, it's also about becoming a son and daughter of God. Remember, you're a **JOINT HEIR!**

You must go through the maturation process, just as Jesus did when He was a child. This is so you can occupy the place God designed for you to occupy. If you would see in the Spirit, you could see the seats alongside of Jesus are empty. One has your name on it, it was predestined before the foundation of the world. It's always been there but because of those blocked places, those areas where you've been bruised or hurt you can't occupy your seat. If you attempted to occupy the seat, the enemy knows those places inside of you that haven't been submitted to God. He knows he has dominion over those areas of your life but, **Jesus is knocking** to set you free! Beloved, we were created to sit in heavenly places with Christ Jesus, far above principalities and powers and rulers. Far above them!

Hebrew 12:2 lets us know the *FINISHED* work of Christ: *"Looking unto Jesus the author and finisher of our faith; who for the joy that was set before him endured the cross, <u>despising the shame</u>, and is set down at the right hand of the throne of God" (KJV).* He conquered it and we can conquer the places where we've been bruised. He was our example and because He did it, He was able to sit down at the right hand of the throne of God. That's where God is calling us to be. He's inviting us to come join Him and occupy our prepared seat in the prepared place. He's calling us to maturity to conquer the shame, abuse, wounds and disappointments of our past. Jesus being our example has already done it and so can we. All we have to do is answer *"THE KNOCK."*

How have you answered the call to maturity?

_____

_____

_____

_____

_____

_____

_____

_____

_____

_____

_____

_____

_____

> *Life comes out of conquering closed doors, it is a sign of spiritual maturity to redefine darkness and call it light...*
> *Minister Tommy Arbuckle*

Prayer

Father, I acknowledge the closed doors and walled off areas within my heart. I make the choice to allow you and Jesus to come in and sup with me. Jesus, I allow you access to every area in my life and I give you the… (*Say the emotion you feel when you think about the event which caused you to not answer "The Knock" for* example: embarrassment, loneliness, guilt, hurt, shame, pain, disappointment, discouragement) from the bruises of my past. I ask that you come and heal the area in my heart that was bruised. Fill it with your love, joy, comfort and peace. I choose today to make an exchange with you to receive my healing and deliverance as part of the maturation process in my life. Jesus, I receive my healing and deliverance. Amen.

After you have said this prayer, check and see if you still have the same negative feeling or maybe a different feeling about the event when you think about it. If you do, just repeat this prayer and say the emotion you now feel about it. Eventually you should feel a complete release of those feelings and end up with total peace from Jesus. Thank you for answering *"The Knock."*

Minister Tommy Arbuckle

References

Bible: New English Translation (NET)

Bible: King James Version

Minister Tommy Arbuckle's personal sermon notes

Quote by Archbishop Mark Dubois

www.dictionary.com

Contact Information

For sharing your testimony as a result of reading this book, request speaking engagements or questions, contact the author at:

Email:

tommyarbuckleministries@gmail.com

Facebook:

https://www.facebook.com/tommyarbuckleministries

YouTube

https://www.youtube.com/@TommyArbuckleMinistries

The

Knock